hello: A collection of poems by a guy who is in love with the idea of being in love.

Kelvin M. Rhodes II

BookLeaf Publishing

India | USA | UK

Presentation by *BookLeaf Publishing*

Web: www.bookleafpub.com

E-mail: info@bookleafpub.com

ISBN:9789360946159

First edition 2024

DEDICATION

I'd like to dedicate this to those I love. Those who have constantly supported me, believed in me and pushed me to be better. Who have read countless drafts of my work. Have liked social posts of my work and have listened to me talk incessantly about writing. This is for y'all.

ACKNOWLEDGEMENT

I'd like to say All Glory Be To God. He blessed me with a talent for writing among many other things. This was a labor of love and Lord knows I prayed many times during this process.

I want to acknowledge my mom, my brother, and my baby sister, I love you. This would not have been possible without your love and support. You never doubted I could do it, even when I doubted myself.

PREFACE

This has been a long time in the making. The number of times I started this project, then walked away for a plethora of reasons, is far more than I would like to admit. But after some gentle urging from someone I consider a personal mentor, another mother, one of my biggest cheerleaders and one of the most generous souls I know, I decided to give it another go.

As the title states I am a guy who is in love with the idea of being in love. I've not ever been in love romantically. I have platonically. I have with food. With art. With music, movies, and tv shows. With pieces of clothing. I've loved people without being in love with them. I have dreamt about it. Thought about it. Longed for it. Pondered it. Been simultaneously intrigued and terrified of it. Some of them will be in your face obvious about love, others will contain snippets of love in various forms. I will start with my earliest poems on the subject and move forward.

Enjoy

Play Hop-skotch Amongst the Lily-Pads

Play Hop-skotch amongst the Lily-Pads
Floating in the sea
Sing atop
The monkey bars
As if you are singing to me
Lean your head back
And stick out your tongue
Catch the falling colors
As they melt into one
Fall back into the waters
Of amber blues and pinks
Feel the mighty brush strokes
As they smooth out the kinks
Touch the sunrise
With your heart and your soul
Trust in its warmth for
It is yours to hold
Smell with your eyes
Taste with your mind
See with your fingers
Listen with your spine
Dodge all the teardrops
Red
Orange

Green
Blue
Relax in my arms
And I will stay dry with you
Play hop-skotch amongst the Lily-pads
Floating in the sea
When we hold hands
I am you and
You are me

Untitled #1

Somewhere
Between
Fiction
And
Desire
Poetry
Will
Sit
Easy
and
Whisper
a
Loud
Dream
for
the
Ancient
Spirits
and
I
Will
Explode
into
Language
More

Vivid
Than
Your
Favorite
Romance
Novel
To
Let
You
Know
I'm
so
Over
Love
and
Magic

Make Your Move

I will
Make you look great
Feel like royalty
Feel love to the depths of your being
Feel safe in my arms
Make you feel like you are all the world
Needs
Wants
Cares about
Deserves
But the things I could do to you are so much
Better
Hotter
Steamier
Sexier
Unbelievably enticing
I could make you weak in the knees with a touch
Make you stop in your tracks with a look
Make you catch your breath with a word uttered
on a breath
I could make you want to
Touch me
Hold me
Kiss me
Claim me

Tickle me
Lick me
Breath
For me
With me
Into me
Make you
Claw in pleasure for whatever you could reach
I could make you do all that with
One move
Now…
Make your move

With My Words

I have my words back
They are flowing like liquid
They just keep coming
Spilling over like a fountain of
Magic
Wonder
Creation
There is nothing stopping them
No barriers
No dividers
No fences
No anything to hold them back, hold me back
It's as if I can breathe with my mind
I have my words again
I have my words to
Live with
Talk to
Converse with
Travel with
Express myself with
Change the world with
I can leave an audience in awe
I can make their minds
Hop
Skip

And jump to the rhythm of my voice
I can make them simultaneously
Feel my heartbreak and my lust with the flip of a
word
With my words
I can kiss speech sensually
I can put everything on paper and
Let it go
With my words
I can
Seduce you
Love you
Caress you
And
Shag. You. Stupid.
I can make you
Love me
Want me
Crave me
Like the worst drug
I can weave you a web of wonder so complex
You won't see what is coming next
With my words I can change
The world
Change you
Change everything
You know
You thought you knew
You believe

You practice
You want
Need
and
Desire
Because with my words
I am a ringmaster
Of creation
A wizard of fantasy
And a magician
Of untold proportions

If

A simple gaze
A lingering look
An interesting, fleeting thought
You wonder if
I wonder if
Are we both wondering the same if?
If I were in your head
And you in mine would
We both see each other at the same time
Would we both take that same faltering breath
At the moment that our eyes first met
I wonder if it is only I that feels this way
I hope you feel the same way I do
Please see into my thoughts
See my desires
My wants
My needs
Please feel the same way I do
I want you too
I need you too
Because if I see even a glimmer of hope
I will take that risk and jump

Untitled #2

Take a chance
Be brave
Trust that I am worth it
Take a breath
Close your eyes
Jump into this ocean
Be free
Trust your gut
Let the current take you
Don't be scared
Take the plunge; know that I will save you
Here we are
At this point
Shrouded in this mist
Trust yourself
Believe me
This is not a miss
We've both been hurt
Used and abused by those we thought to trust
But you know and I know
That this is more than lust
I see your nerves
I feel your fear
I share your apprehension
Let go of your past

I'll do the same
Let's be each other's exception

Paladin

I don't actually know you
As in we haven't met
But you know me
What I desire
What I crave
My Moods. Insecurities
Faults. Fears. Shortcomings
And you are there for me
Despite them
You're my Paladin
Strong. Swift. Fearless.
Facing down the serpents
Deconstructing the walls
Wading through the waves
You face the storm to save the guy

Untitled #3

Foolish
Hopes
And
Dreams
Shrouded
In
Childish
Desires
Get
Quickly
Crushed
By
Harsh
Realities
Of
Grown-up
Responsibilities
And
Selfish
Agendas
Of
Ignorant
Fools
Afraid
Of

Endless
 Possibilities

Urge

I have this urge to reach out to you
And let you into my world
To touch you
To hug you
Embrace you
Hold you
Because I am craving human contact
And I want it to be you
I want to feel your skin on my skin
Your head on my chest
Your hands on my back pulling me to you
Your breath on my face
On my neck
In my ear telling me it's okay
I've got you and I am not letting go
Saying I am here and I will catch the pieces
If you fall apart; I will hold you when you
Are scared and cold and insecure
Because to me you are enough
To me you are equal parts
Confident
And
Sweet
With enough pizazz to make the world
Take notice

And enough heart to be great

Fucked

Fucked upward
Downward. Sideways
Fucked every which way possible
But not a good fucked
Not a toes curling
Heart pounding
Hands gripping
Stars seeing
Lung screaming fucked
More like a
Head spinning
Thoughts racing
Worlds jumping
So flustered you scream
And nothing comes out, fucked
That kind of fucked that makes
A man drink
The kind of fucked that makes the world stop
turning
Makes every sound silent
Except that voice in your head
That says
Fuck
Damn
Hell

Why??
What??
How??
When??
This fucked is so hurtful
It's the type that makes
All your confidence
Blow away in the intensity
Of the fuck
This is the type of fuck
That leaves your mind
Numb
Your soul
Raw
Your emotions
Scattered and Shattered
This fuck makes you
Never want to fuck again

I Want

I want to know you
I know I shouldn't
But that does not change my mind
It should
I wish it did
I want it too
But still, I want to know you

Do you want to know me??
Do you know that you shouldn't??
I am not good for you.
For you I am potent
Unhealthy
Dangerous
I am kryptonite to you
Sucking your strength
Weakening your defenses
Making you something tangible
To each other we are toxic.
Oxygen to a flame.
Two things that are
Majestic. Beautiful when apart.
But together we don't mix

I want to know you
Do you want to know me??
Well, that can't happen
We must stay apart
Be opposite of each other in every aspect
While awake; While asleep
We cannot even meet in a dreamland
Because that would make that sacred place; the
land of our dreams
Barren. Raw. Exposed

Yes, I want to know you
I only hope you want to know me
But it cannot go beyond want; farewell to you
Imagine my kisses on your heart
My hugs in your memories
My touch in your being
And make your life without me…magnificent

You

Sometimes you meet someone
And it all clicks
Slides into place like the lock on a door
Their eyes catch you
Stop you, call you forward
Their voice echoes in your insides
Like memories of old
Their touch on your skin
Reaches through to your soul
Reshapes who you are
Leaving a permanent imprint on your being
They change you so monumentally
So cataclysmically that
You find yourself
Brave. Vulnerable. And foolish
In a single breath
You fight against it
Run from it
Deprive yourself of it
But when you meet someone like this
They catch you. They change you. They impact
you.

Meet Me at the Playground

Meet me at the playground
We'll be kids again
Starting with the Merry-Go Round
Holding hands as we spin
Next we climb the Jungle Gym
Racing to the top
Next to one another
Our fun doesn't stop

Race you to the slide
I think I can beat you there
To the top then to the bottom
Swiftly through the air

On to the swings now
We slowly head over
Bumping shoulders curiously
Briefly glancing over

You push me to the sky
Higher than I've ever been
Instead of being terrified
I just laugh and grin

See-saws were my favorite
I would pretend I could surf
This used to be my sacred space
But now it's our turf

Slowly you walk up to me
The world begins to fade
My eyes meet your eyes
Our feet begin to sway

My arms bring you close to me
Your scent wraps me tight
Your lips on mine desperately
I'm sure we are quite the sight

Your kisses break me down
In the best way ever
So it looks as if the playground; was a
worthwhile endeavor

The Gate

Do you hear me calling you?
Feel my longing within
My voice is just a whisper
Rustling on the wind

Though we've never met
You know me like no other
We live our lives separately
Yet linked to one another

You know when I'm hurting
I know when you are sad
The pull within is so deep
That I fear what we could have

I'm sure that you are it
The one I'm meant to be with
That when I think of meeting you
My world tilts on its axis

You've always given hope to me
Pushed me toward my dreams
Believed in me endlessly
With every fiber of your being

I know that you are out there
Thinking of me
Well don't you worry darlin'
We are destined to be

When we finally meet
The world, it's gonna freeze
And everything we've dreamt about
Will finally come to be

Please don't give up on me
I promise I'm worth the wait
I won't give up on you
I'll be waiting at the gate

Fear

i see you….He thought
you matter….He muttered
i LIKE you….He whispered
but no one replied
not because they didn't care
but because no one heard him
from behind his fear

Frayed

Frazzled. Crackling.
Burning edges. Jagged points
Senses suffocating their hosts
Making them the unwilling ball
In a ping pong match between
Bright. Sharp. Stinging. Loud. Senses
Fighting futilely for dominance…..this is my
sensory overload.
With it my fear that this
Jittery. Short tempered. Incapacitated me.
Who right then, in that moment
Aches longingly. Desperately. Overwhelmingly.
For human contact AND total isolation
Never finds the love that can provide both

You??

Heart racing
Breath catching
Senses ablaze
Lust??

Veins thrumming
Blood pulsing
Thoughts flitting
Passion??

Face blushing
Ears ringing
Back arching
Desire??

Body relaxes
Soul settles
Fears dissipate
…..You??

You!!
Your presence. Your proximity Your practicality
When my insecurities inscribe
Dark damaging verses of vicious words
And atrocious actions

Into my
Mood. Touch. Interactions. Thoughts.
Your Practiced. Persistent. Patient.
Practicality
Makes my
Body relax. Soul settle. Fears dissipate.

It

It comes in many statements
Drive safe
Buckle up
Sweet dreams

It comes in many questions
Are you hungry??
How are you feeling??
Did you sleep well??

It comes in many offers
I'll cook
Let's do what you want
You can sleep in…I've got it.

Drive safe. Buckle up. Sweet dreams.
Are you hungry??
How are you feeling??
Did you sleep well??
I'll cook. Let's do what you want.
You can sleep in….I've got it.
AKA….I love you.

The Worst

We crave it
They say
Nicotine. Alcohol. Opioids
Are the most
Powerful. Addictive. Dangerous.
Substances on earth
But love isn't mentioned.
Studies of what happens to humans
When they aren't touched via
Hugs. Kisses. Slaps on the back.
Slow dancing with loved ones
Held in the arms of people while
Sleeping. Crying. Laughing. Or just being.
Aren't common knowledge to the world at large
Because not being held.
Kissed. Danced with.
Because not being
Loved
Cherished
Honored
Needed
Is the most
Gut-wrenching. Soul-slaughtering.
Way to be…conquered.

hello

The hello of his dreams
Grounded him
Like a familiar hug
Fierce. Intentional. Warm.
As if saying
I'm here. We're here.
I'm not letting go
Until then….hello was merely a word
Now it was the word
Their word. Their I love you
The only thing left to do
Find the owner of his dreamt I love you.

Worth It (Seams)

I know you're out there.
Living. Laughing. Putting love into the world.
Waiting for someone to share all
Your love with.
The someone that will share their love.
That will
Protect you.
Honor you.
Be in awe of how
Someone as magnificent
As simply beautiful
As full of love as you
Could want to share your love
With them. Cherish them. See them
As worth it.
Even on their worst days
Days they are vibrating apart at the
Seams.
Cracking into
Jagged.
Crooked.
Sharp shrapnel that causes them to
Retreat. Hide. Shut down.
Someone that struggles to understand
That no matter how bad it is

You'll always be there
In full battle gear
Armed with superglue and duct tape
To put them back together at the seams
I know you're out there
We'll meet somewhere. Sometime. Someday
And the wait will have been worth it.

I

Bloody Hell I miss you.
Deeply. Achingly. Truly.
It's a hole inside.
Hollow, like a piece scooped out,
Empty, yet full of
Longing.

Loneliness; not to be mistaken with alone
Damn it I want you here
In front of me
Beside me
Embracing me
Letting me crack and crumble
Putting me back together

Fuck, I miss it.
Being cared for without having to ask
Being forced to take a step back
Given no choice, but to self-heal
Pour love back into myself
Allowed to sleep
Honestly sleep. Restfully sleep.
While you cook,
While you remind me to eat.
While you make sure I hydrate

I just.
I want.
…..Please…..
I know life isn't fair
Lord in heaven I know
But it doesn't make it easier
I say all of this
Write all of this
Pour all of this out

Yet I've had this, a version of this
A part of this outside of family
Outside of doctors….Once
And you had to leave
Were forced to choose
I would not; could not let you chose me
You're the closest thing to
Falling in love I've ever had
And I miss it; I miss you

Self Love

Start at the top and work your way down
Start with the physical then move to
Emotional.
Mental.
Spiritual.
My hair. Its texture. Its color.
My eyes. Their shade. The sparkle

My face. The shape of my nose.
The fullness of my lips.
The coarseness of my beard
My long arms. Muscled. Sinewy.
My hands, with long bony fingers.
My long legs.
My groin, where nerves are damaged
And trauma is stored
My brain. Sharp. Equal parts logical and artistic.
Quick. Sees things, adjusts on the fly.
My faith. Large. Loud. Wavering, but strong.
My heart though bruised and scarred is
Compassionate. Loving. Empathetic.
My drive. Determination. Resiliency.
The fight to get up. Keep moving.
Pushing through. Dragging myself on the floor.
Then up to crawling.

Dragging one foot. Then limping.
Walking upright. Skipping. Jogging.
And eventually a full sprint.
Swinging my dreams in the form of whatever
weapon
Needs to be used.
Wielding my scars like a shield.
Because in battle shields get
Cut. Chopped. Burned.
Dented. Bruised. Stepped on.
Kicked. Thrown. But they keep holding up.
Even when they splinter. When they break.
Some piece, still holds up
I still hold up
Acknowledging all the things
I love about myself
It's hard
But…worth it

www.ingramcontent.com/pod-product-compliance
Lightning Source LLC
LaVergne TN
LVHW021314200726
843509LV00012B/1911